ONE MAN'S RAILWAY

O Gauge in the Garden

Allen Jackson

AMBERLEY

Author's Note

There are numerous references in the text to commercially available products and I would like to make it clear that I have no connection with the producers of these products other than that of customer.

There are references to electrical mains-operated equipment and I would advise anyone to follow the manufacturer's safety instructions and if in doubt to seek qualified help.

First published 2021

Amberley Publishing
The Hill, Stroud,
Gloucestershire, GL5 4EP

www.amberley-books.com

ISBN: 978 1 3981 0764 9 (print)
ISBN: 978 1 3981 0765 6 (ebook)

British Library Cataloguing in Publication Data.
A catalogue record for this book is available from the British Library.

Typeset in 10pt on 13pt Celeste.
Typesetting by Amberley Publishing.
Printed in the UK.

Contents

CHAPTER 1

A Potted History

1950–58

I was born in York and my family initially moved to what was then Malaya where my father fought the communist terrorists in the Malayan Emergency. On our return we lived in a two-up two-down terraced house in York, now demolished, which had an outside toilet and tin bath in the kitchen but no whippets.

The most abiding early memory, of around five years old, is my dad fitting a cushion secured with string to the crossbar of his Raleigh bike (green with chain guard and Sturmey Archer 3 speed gears and dynamo lights) to enable me to ride with him to Leeman Road to visit the pathway by the north engine sheds, now the York base of the National Railway Museum. Our favourite location was right by the 'cenotaph' coaling plant where engines were perpetually moving in and out for coal and, if you were lucky, you could see a 16-t mineral wagon loaded with coal ascending up the side of the coaling plant to tip its load. A massive cloud of dust accompanied a successful tip, although water was sprayed to keep the dust down. At the coaling plant you could also see the yard, where there would be sixty to seventy engines in steam, and the East Coast Main Line where a procession of trains to and from the north would be running slowly, threading their way through the point work past the sheds and carriage sidings. We would then go past the coaling stage to the turntable at the bottom of the yard where interlopers like Royal Scots, Patriots or Jubilees would be stabled before their usual return west and south. It wasn't trainspotting then as such, just an interest in trains or engines.

The paternal grandfather was a platelayer on the LNER in the 1930s and we visited his home at station house Eryholme Junction on the East Coast Main Line. The A4, A3, A2 and A1 Pacifics would hurtle past the bedroom window, a few feet away, and make the room shake somewhat more than W. H. Auden's description in the poem 'Night Mail'.

I first got involved in the railway modelling hobby, or perhaps train set, at least at the age of six or seven. I was presented with a Hornby O Gauge Clockwork Train set. This did innumerable circuits around the sitting-room floor. It said 35s (£1.75) on the box. As the sitting room was the holy of holies and hardly ever used there were occasions when the train set could be left on the floor complete with a cereal box cardboard platform.

Next was an upgrade to electricity, although not very much of it. The nearest model shop was a Trix Twin dealer in Fossgate and so a 6-v train set was purchased for around £3. We had moved to No. 145 Lawrence Street in York by this time, which is a large Victorian house, and I was given the drawing room for trains and the dining room as a bedroom, although neither were used for their intended designations.

The supplied oval of track was extended each week as the pocket money stipend of 2s 6d (12½ pence) was just enough to buy two pieces of Trix Twin Universal straight track. Merit plastic trees and Airfix kits in the shape of the platform and station building and a footbridge were assembled and placed on the floor along with the track. I think a 1/76th scale Airfix Spitfire also made an appearance in the trees. The 6-v Distler DC motor didn't have much go in the 0-4-0 tank engine, which would scarcely pull the two coaches in the set, so an upgrade to 12 v was needed. My father said that anything I saved up he would double. I appalled him by saving £3 10s (£3.50), which to his credit he honoured, although that was then around half a week's wages.

1959–62

This budget strengthening enabled a Trix 12-v DC LNER Hunt Class 4-4-0 numbered 62750 and called 'The Pytchley' after the famous one in Leicestershire. My more discerning eyes noticed that what should have been the large driving wheels on the engine were basically the same diameter as on the small 0-4-0 tank of the 6-v era. Also, the coupling rod wasn't actually attached to the front driving wheels. Still, it went well and would comfortably outpace most other OO-gauge engines of the period. An important consideration then. Trix had famously been 20 v AC in a previous era, a harbinger of DCC perhaps.

The other half of the sketch was a Hammant & Morgan 12-v Safety Minor power supply and controller, which was considered the acme of electrical sophistication then with its variable transformer speed controller that was superior to the resistance mat type. The short-circuit cut out was a manually resettable red button, which added to the fascination of something else to control and an audible warning something was wrong.

To 1959 and a move to a modern bungalow on the outskirts north of York and within sound of the East Coast Main Line – the distant sound of steam-hauled expresses speeding north or south.

My dad was often too busy with work to spend any time on the model railway, but one day he announced that a chap at the factory had a 5-ft by 3-ft baseboard to give away, and it was even painted green. This was eventually struggled home lashed to the side of the push bike and set up in my bedroom using two old chairs as legs.

This baseboard enabled a double-track formation and by now a Trix GWR 56XX had been bought as a combined birthday and Christmas present, together with the plastic-bodied goods wagons collected over time. The Trix Twin system featured the control of two trains on one track. As it was three rail, one outside rail was the pickup and the centre rail was the common return. They later introduced the LNER EM1 Bo-Bo, which had overhead catenary for the Woodhead line 1,500 v DC of the prototype. This meant three trains on one track, individually controlled – one of the features of DCC systems in the twenty-first century and about as useful then as now in practical terms.

The Hunt 4-4-0 acquired some of the Trix 'scale' coaches, which were tinplate but had lights from a pickup system that needed the voltage to be turned up fairly high for noticeable illumination.

After a short time of this an 8-ft by 4-ft board was purchased in softboard – then used as a kind of insulating board, I think, in the building industry. This needed a 2-in by 1-in pine frame, which I think Dad did with my help.

The trackwork was developed into a single oval this time with an extensive Trix station with overall roof, and a GWR motive power depot consisting of a Hornby Dublo two-road engine shed and an Airfix engine shed with extension – 6s for two kits, or 30p now. The loco stud now included 3 Trix 56XX 0-6-2T, Britannia and Standard Class 5 in green, Warship diesel, Hornby Dublo Three-rail Castle (7032 Denbigh) and 48158 LMS 2-8-0, all for £2 2s (£2.10), which was around half price then in a sale at Precious in Petergate York. The three-rail Hornby Dublo engines had to have a special isolation section when not in use as they would short out the two outside running rails. This wouldn't matter on Hornby Dublo track, but did on Trix Twin Universal track.

A Triang Jinty LMS 0-6-0T was acquired and that had to be three railed – an early engineering exercise and a surprisingly successful one.

As the LMS was making a multiple appearance a separate depot was constructed by a pal from card and brick paper, which looked quite realistic. A bit like the depots I was tramping round at weekends recording steam on its way out, only smaller in both senses. The track was also ballasted with granite chippings as opposed to the Peco foam underlay. This was a scenic enclave in what had been an enlarged train set and a dissatisfaction set in.

Also, the *Railway Modeller* had been delivered to the bungalow we moved to since October 1959 and I could see some of the work of George Iliffe Stokes and Peter Denny, which made me realise there were other possibilities that didn't necessarily need a large budget.

Another aspect of modelling not hitherto included was signalling. Trix had developed colour light signals that used a refractive plastic tube to convey the light to the head. A switch was needed to select different coloured bulbs or, more correctly, the same type of bulb with a different colour piece of tissue paper laid over it.

Into this system they had placed a means of placing a large filament bulb at the switch. When placed in circuit with an ON or red signal selection it would slow the train down quite realistically and, with care in initial speed selection, bring the train to a stand at the then red signal. This was an early form of AWS (Automatic Warning System) in model form, albeit it worked on the home signal rather than the distant as in the prototype.

A soldering iron had been acquired and the mysteries of the skill slowly revealed themselves.

1963–87

In around 1963 there was a change to Graham Farish 2 rail and a GWR branch terminus to fiddle yard. Building began on K's loco kits with a GWR 2-6-0 63XX Mogul.

I later joined the RAF as an aircraft apprentice. I was involved in RAF Halton Model Railway Club layout and partook of exhibiting it at an RAF show. The untimely demise of my parents on separate occasions meant that the branch line railway had to be broken up and the stock sold in the *Railway Modeller* classifieds.

Years later, after marriage and a family start in 1976, I joined RAF Sealand Model Railway Club and with one other member, a certain John Burnett, took part of the club layout off the system and built a fiddle yard and exhibited that in eight weeks. We started with working signals for the 1977 season. The layout was called Ashbridge – Ashburton and Kingsbridge cobbled together.

Its successor was built by later club members until it was Railway of the Month in the *Railway Modeller* in December 1982, still named Ashbridge.

In 1979, I created a layout called Torcross, which was 4 mm, 2 ft by 18 ft and extended to 2 ft by 24 ft and 6 in after a year – a Devonian seaside terminus to fiddle yard. Working signals and interlocked with points and block bells (scratch built), working scratch-built turntable, hand-built track including three-way point of mostly K's and Wills loco kits, and kit-built wagons (fifty odd) but adapted and modified proprietary coaches.

At home it ran between two buildings with a bridging piece put in and this created the separation and notion that trains were going to somewhere and from somewhere.

Figure 01. RAF Sealand open day, 9 September 1978, and a carefully posed shot by an RAF cameraman of the original exhibition layout Ashbridge. (MOD Crown Copyright)

Figure 02. Ashbridge in operation the same day as above. All trains came into the platform as the loop hadn't yet been signalled. There was no sequence, but the fiddle yard operator varied the running and indicated on a series of cards what was next. The station building and overall roof were scratch built, but the engine shed and signal box were Prototype Models kits.

Figure 03. Torcross Signal Box, a Churchward Models kit, with interior and lights. The lampman is attending to the oil store and the filling of lamps. Some attempt was made to create signal wires. The track and points were handmade. The layout was fully signalled but none of them were lit. (1984)

Figure 04. Torcross station from the viewing side. Wills kit 51XX GWR large prairie waits for the carriage shunter to bring the coaches into the platform. Another go at a Brunel overall roof – 4,000 'slates' this time. (1984)

Figure 05. Torcross turntable is lined up to let GWR Bulldog 4-4-0 Sir Watkin Wynn, a modified K's kit, pointing in the right direction for Exeter. The turntable deck was made of copper clad with a slot in the middle. The pickup was from the circular track. This meant the supply polarity always remained in sync when the locomotive was turned. It also meant the track was short-circuited while a loco was turning, which was a useful feature. Power is by geared electric motor. (1985)

Figure o6. Torcross tunnel mouth signal, which marked the changeover electrically between the station and fiddle yard. The signal was interlocked with the fiddle yard controller, who had to select 'Torcross' as opposed to 'fiddle yard' before the signal would come off. This meant the Torcross controller drove the train into the fiddle yard. The engine shed is basically Bodmin. (1984)

Figure o7. Red Damsel is a superb piece of engineering from Tolhurst Model Engineers and would operate from gas or coal; there was even a methylated spirit cassette for those of that persuasion. It's got working Stephenson's valve gear between the frames. (2004)

The layout ran for eight years successfully; it all worked reliably. The layout was sold in 1989 to a millionaire computer system dealer, Tony Thomas, who had been a signaller in a previous life at Bridgnorth on what is now the Severn Valley Railway. He'd seen the layout at the Wolverhampton exhibition.

By 1987 I had left the RAF and worked for an international computer systems company. By this time the lure of real steam had got me and I was into garden steam railways and scratch built eight garden railway battery diesel locos, seven of which were sold. I wrote the first one up for *16 mm Today* magazine over three installments. I also wrote various articles on signalling, bridges and such like.

Figure 08. The garden railway and the John Turner 'Gelert' gas-fired live steamer romps away with kit-built Welshpool and Llanfair Light Railway goods rolling stock. (September 2003)

Figure 09. The first battery diesel scratch built was this model of the Festiniog Railway Upnor Castle, as seen running on John Murray's line. (Photo by Bobby Hine, who also built the slate wall. 1995)

CHAPTER 2

A Tentative O Gauge Restart

The pensions bombshell was dropped in 2003 where the announcement was made that I would get around one fifth of that estimated. Shortly afterwards I formed my own business to try and get some of my money back.

Thoughts of a plan of an O-gauge layout started ruminating and while Torcross had been a Devon seaside resort with the emphasis on passenger trains and excursions, its O-Gauge successor was to be quite different.

The North Wales Mineral Railways had sought to extract first lead and then coal, lime and ironstone from an area west of Wrexham, which itself was a centre for the north-east Wales coal industry.

An ironworks had been established at Brymbo, which continued in production until 1990. A bridge over the road at Tan-y-Bwlch on the Ffestiniog Railway bears an inscription for Brymbo to this day.

Prototype Involvement and History

The Wrexham Mold & Connah's Quay Railway serviced this area and docks around the River Dee and later became part of the Great Central Railway, which was a constituent of the LNER.

The GWR was pre-eminent in Wrexham and had a double-track branch line to Brymbo steelworks that generated massive traffic in limestone, coal, coke, ironstone and finished steel products. The line only closed in 1982; it was a result of a steel strike and railway unions blocking the line's operation in support of the strikers. After that it all went by road.

The London & North Western Railway, later LMS sought to get into the lucrative minerals act with a branch line from their Chester to Denbigh line, starting at Mold, through Coed Talon and on to Brymbo. The part from Coed Talon onwards was joint with the GWR. The LNWR were unsuccessful and the line remained a bucolic country branch line and closed early but was incorporated into the model.

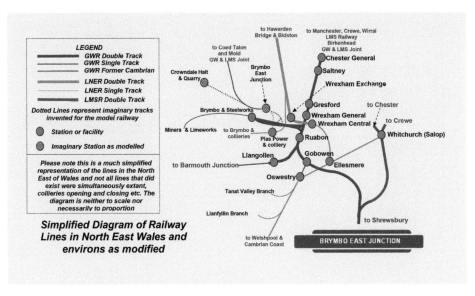

Simplified Diagram of Railway Lines in North East Wales and environs as modified

to Hawarden Bridge & Bidston

to Manchester, Crewe, Wirral
LMS Railway
Birkenhead
GW & LMS Joint

to Coed Talon and Mold
GW & LMS Joint

Chester General

Brymbo East Junction

Saltney

Crowndale Halt & Quarry

Wrexham Exchange

Brymbo & Steelworks

Gresford   to Chester

Wrexham General

Wrexham Central   to Crewe

Minera & Limeworks   to Brymbo & collieries

Plas Power & colliery

Ruabon

Whitchurch (Salop)

Llangollen

Gobowen

to Barmouth Junction

Ellesmere

Oswestry

Tanat Valley Branch

Llanfyllin Branch

to Shrewsbury

to Welshpool & Cambrian Coast

BRYMBO EAST JUNCTION

Figure 10. A simplified diagram of the railways around Wrexham and Brymbo, as modified for the Brymbo East Junction model.

Model Interpretation

So, these small railway workings were home to three of the Big Four, and that gave some railway diversity and interest. Brymbo East Junction never existed, but on the layout it connects the steelworks and Wrexham General station (GWR) with Plas Power Colliery (LNER), with a branch line to Crowndale Halt (joint GWR and LMS). The principal traffic is coal from the colliery to the steelworks and consequent empties from the steelworks back to the colliery. There are pickup goods of GWR and LMS origin and a steel products train once a sequence.

Each operator has their own controller and signals where appropriate and the fiddle yard has two controllers. A train can leave the fiddle yard on Controller Two, but after around 15 ft, or a decent headshunt length, it enters a dead zone whereupon Controller One takes over, using a push button to enliven the first part of the section. After that the train can be set to run on its own down the 1 in 60 until it enters the changeover/handover point. The train will come into view again for all operators on Camera 6. The train's progress can be monitored or, perhaps more precisely, heard using the microphone and loudspeaker. A train setting off is a distant but increasing sound until it passes the midpoint where the microphone is and where the specially cut track joints make it sound like a real train, then the sound tails off as it makes its way to the branch point. A similar sequence is had on the way up the gradient towards the fiddle yard, but in this case a train will automatically come to a stand in the Controller One dead zone, leaving the fiddle yard operator the time to carry out shunting while the journey is underway and not worry about the train's imminent arrival. Camera 7 will provide visual confirmation the train has arrived as well as the Controller 1 ammeter indicating zero.

Before some of the construction of the layout is looked at the track layout is produced on a series of diagrams.

13

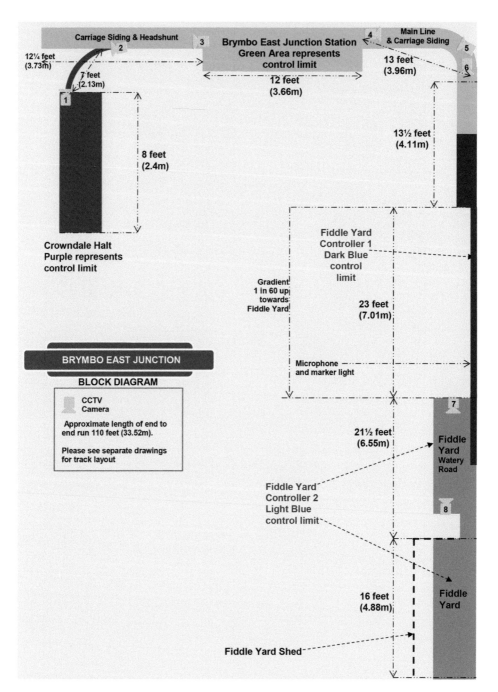

Figure 11 is an overview of the layout in block form showing the areas of control: one operator for each differently coloured area and each operator has their own CCTV cameras to cover that area of control. The views from the cameras are duplicated to some extent such that the Crowndale Halt operator, for example, sitting in the purple area in that shed, can see the changeover/handover point view from Camera 6 between the blue and green areas. This gives the Crowndale Halt operator advance warning that a train bound for that shed is on its way. A pair of binoculars is also provided in the Crowndale Halt shed.

Figure 12 shows Crowndale Halt on the left and the main line curves round to join the carriage siding and headshunt before entering Brymbo East Junction shed at the left. It re-emerges past the workman's carriage siding to the junction itself, which has the large flat piece of polycarbonate roofing in the right-hand corner, before curving around some more with the two single lines of GW and GC (LNER). Just by the dwarf Cyprus tree and the start of the wooden fence panels the line goes back into single track to climb the 1 in 60 up to the fiddle yard. (March 2020)

Figure 13 shows the camera pointing back at the house and the rest of the journey up the gradient on the dark blue section to Watery Road Yard, where the single track becomes five and a short distance after that is the fiddle yard shed itself. The single-line trackbed is secured to the concrete fence posts as well as supported by wooden posts. On the single line and in the yard, the lid of the polycarbonate is hinged to gain access to track and stock. (March 2020)

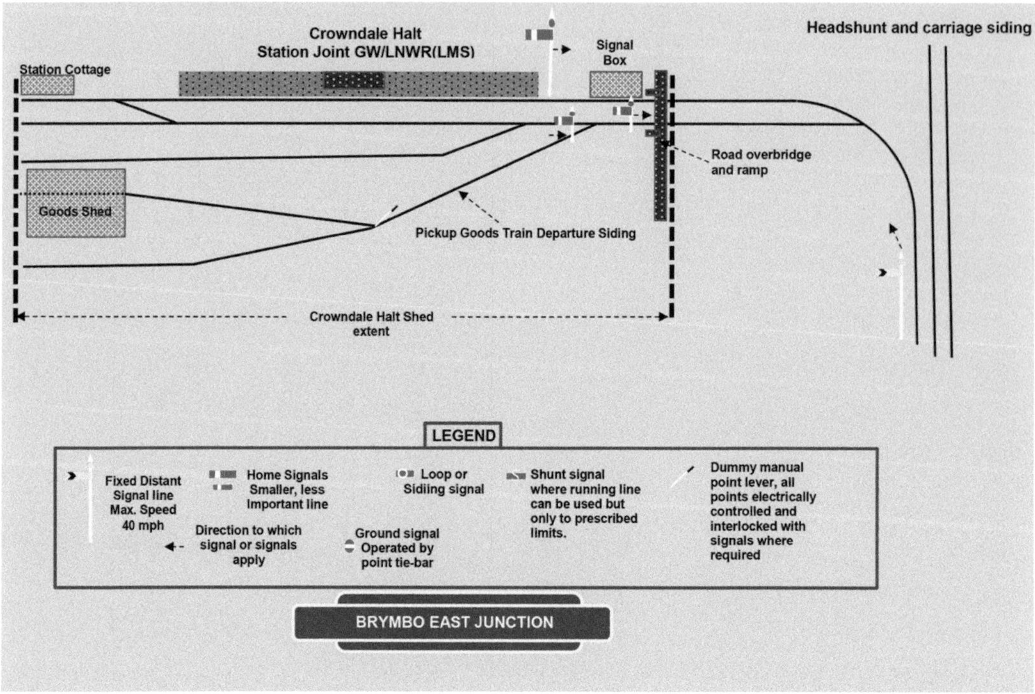
Crowndale Halt
Station Joint GW/LNWR(LMS)
Signal Box
Headshunt and carriage siding
Station Cottage
Goods Shed
Road overbridge and ramp
Pickup Goods Train Departure Siding
Crowndale Halt Shed extent
LEGEND
Fixed Distant Signal line Max. Speed 40 mph
Home Signals Smaller, less Important line
Direction to which signal or signals apply
Loop or Sidiing signal
Ground signal Operated by point tie-bar
Shunt signal where running line can be used but only to prescribed limits.
Dummy manual point lever, all points electrically controlled and interlocked with signals where required
BRYMBO EAST JUNCTION

Above: Figure 14. Crowndale Halt track layout. In a 7-ft by 8-ft shed in O gauge the run round point has to be outside the shed to ensure three coaches can be run round. The shed is on the extreme left of the garden overview at Figure 12.

A conventional small terminus with limited goods yard facilities. The small signal indicates the freight departure road as using the loop line would inhibit a passenger train running round. Both smaller signals are interlocked with the throat point, as is the platform starter signal. There should be a bracket signal on the way into the station and that will get built at some point. Crowndale Halt is the only place on the layout where goods train shunting takes place. The coal trains and empties at Brymbo East Junction are merely turned around. There are two LMS pickup goods and one GWR pickup in the sequence. There is a dedicated yard shunter and a spare loco is provided. There are two complete trains here at the beginning of a sequence: the Sunday school excursion and the LMS pickup goods.

Opposite above: Figure 15. Brymbo East Junction shed track layout on the original two baseboards. The signalling must seem a bit confusing, but it is only what is required for a single-track branch line and although a couple of ground disks have been modelled, there would have been several in reality. The two sidings at the bottom of the board inside the shed are for waiting coal trains. The bay platform is for the Plas Power Autotrain and a van train for the loading dock. The workman's carriage siding just accommodates three four-wheeled coaches and a tank locomotive. All of the shed's thirteen controllable signals are controlled by the Brymbo East Junction operator and each line out – that is GW/LMS to Crowndale Halt, GW to Wrexham (fiddle yard) and LNER to Plas Power (fiddle yard) – has its own set of block instruments. There are four complete trains here at the beginning of a sequence.

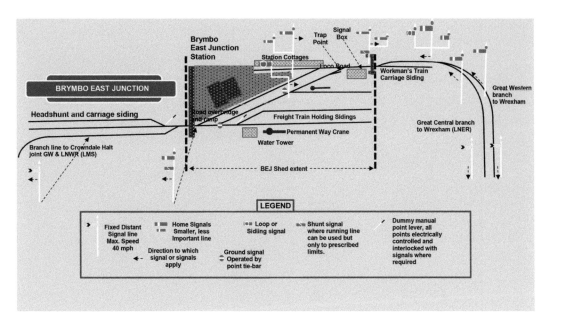

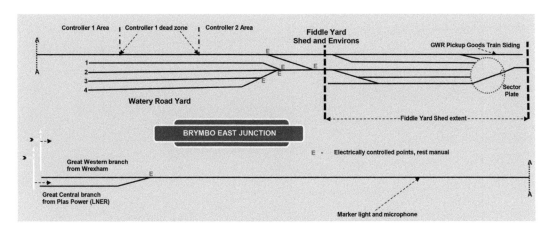

Figure 16 is the final destination and originating point for all trains: the fiddle yard.

The fiddle yard operator has two controllers; while this may seem like a burden it actually makes life easier, giving time to shunt the yard while a train is on its way to or from the yard.

Each of the numbered sidings can hold two complete standard trains and the loop lines inside the shed similarly but of lesser length. The sector plate siding and headshunt can accommodate light engines or an autotrain and the GWR pickup siding is limited to eight wagons plus tank locomotive.

There are no working signals here but there are two sets of block instruments.

There are ten complete trains here at the beginning of the sequence and they all fit inside the shed when we are not running.

Passenger traffic was an early casualty in the Brymbo area in the 1930s, but here on the model it has survived and is thriving. There are even excursions to the North Wales holiday resorts via the GWR to Barmouth and via Chester and the LMS to Llanberis.

The rest of the GWR and LNER systems end up at the fiddle yard, which has expanded to be a considerable stock-handling operation to give the variety and interest needed. The LMS trains from Crowndale Halt access home territory through the LNER through Plas Power to Wrexham Central, with more imaginary meanderings to Whitchurch (Shropshire) over the former Cambrian lines and hence to Crewe. Indeed, some of these routes were used to bypass Crewe during the Second World War to escape the bombing.

The period depicted is around 1936, with all three companies in operation, although the line slips into nationalised mode (c. 1968) for diesel nights where a much-reduced service is run, and the Crowndale Halt branch line has had the Beeching Axe.

The line can run in two-shed mode if there are not three operators available, which happens occasionally. The line is run to a sequence of fifty moves, which is truncated to forty-two moves in two-shed mode. Of the fifty moves with three sheds, the Crowndale Halt branch line sees eighteen of the total.

There are twenty locomotives to handle the 1936 traffic, with five spares and seven green diesels including a single railcar for the 1968 BR version.

At this point the operating philosophy emerged where a train would disappear from view on its journey to somewhere else, just like the real ones do, and an operator would be

Figure 17 is an example of such excursion traffic: a train has arrived on the GW branch from Wrexham General to pick up passengers and then returns up the GW to go through to Chester. No. 4588 has an express passenger headcode – not that it is speedy, but instead will perform limited stops. The elderly Dean clerestory coaches were in regular use at this time but not on top expresses. (December 2019)

Figure 18. The fiddle yard shed contents and Watery Road Yard can just be glimpsed outside the shed. (August 2013)

required for each destination. The operator would be a train driver and a signaller passing a train from one section to the next under proper railway-like control using the Absolute Block system pioneered in the mid-nineteenth century and still used in 2020 in some places, although adapted for single-line use. While trains were on their way to somewhere else some degree of control would be exercised by CCTV and where there were shunting moves outside the sheds at carriage sidings and so forth.

The business had got even busier and so a halt was called to further outside works, which were not resumed until summer 2010. Also at this point, the other end of the shed had a simple headshunt.

The original shed is at a level below the house and the fiddle yard shed. This meant that in roughly 60 ft the track had to climb around a foot to maintain fiddle yard boards at the same height as the main shed.

A 1 in 60 gradient on the real thing and the model is considerable and rolling stock will run down that slope unassisted.

The 1 in 60 gradient section is not under CCTV surveillance, which I feel enhances the feeling of distance and a journey travelled. There is a microphone halfway; it is a mobile phone earpiece whose signal is amplified and played on a loudspeaker in the fiddle yard. This way the operator can hear the train approaching the fiddle yard shed or leaving it from the point it leaves CCTV coverage.

CHAPTER 3

Some Constructional Detail

The purpose of this chapter is to illustrate some of the more unusual features of the layout and a good deal of the piece is to do with running outdoors as that is a fairly challenging environment, particularly when you run at all times of the year in the British weather.

In 2006 I started O gauge on two 5-ft boards in the conservatory. I intended to add a fiddle yard and exhibit as had been done with Torcross. The roar of the greasepaint and smell of the crowd, I suppose, but I soon realised the railway would need a lot of boards either side of the two already there and that it would be unwieldy and unmanageable.

Figure 19. The original two baseboards in the conservatory. These would form the basis of the Brymbo East Junction station shed boards. (May 2006)

The baseboards were 2-in by 1-in pine, topped with chipboard – certainly not state of the art, but finances were tight. Although Peco code 124 bullhead track was chosen, the decision was taken to use C&L Finescale points, which being nearer scale – and therefore longer – wouldn't fit on the baseboards in the planned configuration. It was decided to truncate the length of the kit-built points to fit the two baseboards. The geometry of the frogs was to remain the same, which if that seems unlikely to work was proved to be the case, at least reliably. The Brymbo East Junction station had to be relaid with Peco points after a couple of years trying to get the mutilated C&L versions to work. At this point the business also started to get busy, so the railway eye was not on the ball. There was also a false start in trying to get various second-hand point motors to work reliably with a capacitor discharge unit until business picked up and new Fulgurex started to be used.

The two boards left the conservatory and took up residence in the new shed and a bridging piece had to be built as the boards were only 5 ft by 2 ft. Holes were cut into the shed walls so the railway could expand into the garden.

Civil Engineering

On a real railway this refers to bridges, tunnels, earthworks and the creation of an environment such that the railway can run smoothly and safely. It is much the same with O gauge in the garden, except that the problems are different in nature; for example, everything must be squirrel proof. An early excursion into the garden taught me that lesson: one end of the unfinished loop that represents the two branch lines attracted the attention of a squirrel, when it realised it could not turn round it proceeded at breakneck speed, faster than any train, past the branch junction into the tunnel mouth at BEJ. The signals for the end of the platform had just been put in and it miraculously somehow missed these, jumped off the boards and scuttled out of the shed via the open door. Who was the more relieved?

A base for a 12-ft by 8-ft shed was constructed and mains power was run out from the house using armoured cable buried in the garden but following the fence line to avoid digging it up at some point.

The four timber pieces are then screwed or nailed to the posts, and it all has to be levelled up with a spirit level by tapping the posts with a sledgehammer.

The rubble and old bricks form a base for the concrete and you must smash them up and smash them down with a sledgehammer – very satisfying. Then, lengthwise and crosswise, lay steel-reinforcing strips. They can be metal coat hangers, an old bedstead or a steel strip from a steel stockholder who will cut it to length for you.

The amount of concrete has to be calculated and it's a volume thing of metric length by breadth by depth and it has to be in cubic metres as that is how ready mixed concrete is sold. Don't worry if you underestimate as they will just add on a bit to fill up the concrete mould. I think I calculated around half a cubic metre for the Crowndale Halt base of 7 ft by 8 ft. I was less than a barrowload underestimated and I don't think they charged me the extra as they are used to dealing with tonnes at a time.

Choose a ready-mixed concrete firm that advertises they will barrow the concrete from the wagon onto your mould. It is back-breaking work otherwise if you are not used to it,

Figure 20 is actually the base for Crowndale Halt shed but will illustrate the points needed. The four timber pieces are held upright with posts driven in with a pick and spade. If the ground is soft you can bash the posts in gently with a sledgehammer, using a piece of plywood acting as a buffer so the post doesn't split, but I encountered tree roots and the odd stone. (May 2013)

and capsizing wheelbarrows full of sloppy concrete can be an unmitigated disaster. The concrete will take a few hours to 'start to go off' and longer still before it has set hard. Best leave it a couple of days once it is where you want it.

The prevailing winds are left to right and it can get up to 80 mph here, therefore the shed itself and its roof need to be firmly anchored down. Part of this strategy is to bring in the armoured cable around by the gate across the top of the picture and route it round to the left and enter the shed through the floor there. When this is secured it is like an anchor.

The first excursion of the railway into the garden required 3-in square fence posts set into a hole dug around 18 in deep and filled with Postcrete, a quick setting concrete mix sold in a handy bag – just add water. You can ensure the post is vertical by either using a spirit level or a nail at the top of the post with a string attached, on the end of which is a heavy weight or plumb bob. When the string is parallel with the side of the post, it's level.

The first post, which was intentionally too high, was then marked off using a spirit level resting on the shed exit trackbed at one end and the post plus trackbed thickness allowance at the other. The post was then cut to the correct height and the trackbed thus extended and secured using decking screws, which do not seem to rust. This method allowed around three posts per day to be put in.

A large sheet of 1-in thick ply was used for the actual junction trackbed, and it was cut to shape before being screwed to the fence posts. In the early days, from 2006 to 2008, the

Figure 21 is the poured concrete being 'tamped' so that it makes a level with the boards all the way round. This is supposed to be 'One Man's Railway', but there are some things that need a friend to help out. In this case it's Fred Ashley, a stalwart from Torcross days and now the Brymbo East Junction driver/signaller. I'm supposed to be on the other end of the tamper board. With an up and down and sawing motion the concrete is 'worried' into place. (May 2013)

Figure 22 has moved on to baseboard construction and here it is a plywood top donated by another pal, Graeme Davies, who has a large 4-mm layout in a specially built extension. The baseboards are secured to the walls of the shed – this is to strengthen the shed as much as provide track stability. The paving slab is shed ballast to lessen the Starling Bank advert syndrome of an aerial shed. The anchored armoured cable also helps in this regard. Out of shot are the bearers on which the shed roof sits. They are secured to the shed walls and roof with decking screws to lessen aerodynamic tendencies. (May 2013)

outdoor section got only as far as the junction with the two branch lines and ending up at the 'loop' point, which was eventually to be controlled by the fiddle yard.

The multiple track parts outside are plywood bases on a 2-in by 1-in frame. The cross members of the frame are pre-drilled to take some of the cabling that electrically connects the sheds, CCTV, block bells and then local cabling for lights and point motors and relay control. The upright piece where the back scene is was originally ply, but that has now been changed to polycarbonate roofing material cut up as required. The ply delaminated after around ten years.

The roofing is kept at an angle by the vertical piece of 2 by 1, and a hinged door gives access to the track.

To round off this section on civil engineering are two photos that are at the somewhat more humdrum end of the hobby but necessary to keep the railway going.

Figure 23. Outside the Crowndale Halt shed and the posts that hold up the trackbed. The right-hand one has a damp patch at the bottom and in around five to ten years that'll be the place it will rot through. The blue post on the left has the Postcrete 'haunched' up and this process needs to follow through on all posts to minimise rot; this is in addition to the concrete holding the post up in the first place, which is buried below ground. (March 2020)

Figure 24. This is what happens to posts eventually. They are all treated with garden fence paint, which, while decorative, does not seem to prevent the rot much. An earlier technique was to dunk the post in a mixture of creosote and used engine oil; it would last for years but is now environmentally incorrect and messy.

'Tanalised' timber is injected with arsenic and that seems to last a bit longer, but not the twenty-five years they advertise in my experience. No doubt terms and conditions apply.

The single trackbed is tanalised timber from a builder's merchant and, while the width varies depending on how many tracks it carries, the thickness is three-quarters of an inch. This allows screws to go in deeply. Multiple track parts of it are ply. (March 2020)

Figure 25. On one occasion the existing post rotted through enough to allow the trackbed to sag and an additional post (still unpainted) was put in. Both posts had decking screws put in at right angles and more concrete haunched around the posts and screws to lessen any tendency to move. (March 2020)

Figure 26. Polycarbonate roofing as supplied in 10-mm thickness and 2,400-mm sheets from eBay is the staple outdoor cladding material. It is light, strong and yet easily cut. A jigsaw with a fine blade cuts through easily.

The polycarbonate pieces are secured with 'spat roofing washers' (once again from eBay) and these spread the load of the decking screw and washer as shown, as well as seal against water getting in. Some edges of the polycarbonate are covered by edging strips and these are useful where you need to secure a decking screw for the wire coat hanger latch as shown. (March 2020)

Figure 27. Fowler 4F makes its way from Crowndale Halt to Wrexham Central on the GC (LNER), while GWR pickup goods with Sang Cheng 57XX Pannier tank heads on the GWR for Brymbo East Junction and Crowndale Halt. The location is right in front of CCTV Camera 6 – see Figure 11. The back scene and general scenic work have weathered, but this is not noticeable on the monitors in the sheds. (July 2019)

Figure 28. This is a close-up view of the side cover retaining device. It is known as a trailer tailgate latch on eBay and is a quick, easy and secure method of retaining the polycarbonate side door. The handles are the cheaper kitchen cupboard variety and need a washer behind or you end up holding just the handle. I have searched in vain for a top hat bush to place into the polycarbonate to act as a bearing, but they appear to be made to measure and so are hideously expensive. (March 2020)

Figure 29. The vertical piece is slid upward and rotated 90 degrees as shown. The door can then be removed/opened. You have to ensure that you assemble these and tighten them up so that the locking piece is horizontal, as shown. (March 2020)

Figure 30. The ends of the removable polycarbonate doors can bend outwards and let the wind or leaves in. A decking screw with a penny washer can be used to retain the door in place and yet leave the door free to move. The flash banding provides a seal between shed and railway with a piece of plastic channel to act as a gutter. (April 2020)

Figure 31. GWR Mogul 5322 with brake end and B Set coaches forms part of the Sunday school excursion from Crowndale Halt for Barmouth or the fiddle yard. Behind the first coach is the white marker board and ultra-bright LEDs that denote the halfway point between the fiddle yard and the start of the CCTV section that monitors both branch lines. (August 2015)

Figure 32. The mobile phone earpiece acting as a microphone and the wiring extended some 30 ft using ¼-in, 6-mm microphone extension, as used in discos and such like – eBay again. A hefty track joint is just below and there are others nearby to emphasise the sound of a train passing. (March 2020)

Figure 33. The halfway point, as described in Figure 31. The LEDs are permanently lit and at night a train passing obscures their illumination, giving a visual indicator to both Brymbo East Junction and Crowndale Halt that a train is passing. The small cardboard shield secured with drawing pins is to avoid blinding Camera 8 in the fiddle yard. (March 2020)

Figure 34. Watery Road trackbed was built from 75-mm by 20-mm planks connected beneath by more planking. This enabled the yard to be expanded easily from three roads and three trains to four roads and eight trains. However, despite being held down, the planks persist in moving about and track has to be relevelled with cardboard packing. No track is solidly pinned down as that is a derailment generator since the wood moves. (March 2020)

Figure 35. Watery Road Yard follows the 1 in 60 gradient of the main line on the left. This means any stock in the yard stays where it is rather than being blown around if the lids are lifted. Camera 8 is on the back wall of the yard. (March 2020)

Figure 36. The track to Crowndale Halt was at first covered with transparent A4 sheets folded over the trackbed and secured with bulldog clips to enable access. Eventually the sheets split and were replaced with polycarbonate, which does not like cornering. The precursor to this was garden cloches but snow caused an obstruction on the polytunnel-type construction and it was tricky for access. (January 2018)

Figure 37. The fiddle yard is essentially a lean to, with the house wall one long side and the garden fence the other. The garden fence side was boxed in with ¾-in ply sheets – the light-coloured wall is those sheets secured to the garden fence posts. This meant that the fiddle yard trackbed, also ply sheets from the same source, could be secured with angle brackets to the ply and only needed legs at the front of the trackbed as shown. The floor was made of redundant kitchen cupboard doors, which are of oak and were eventually covered in carpet floor tiles.

A Heljan Class 35 Hymek used to prove electrical continuity. All wheel pickup ensures that you know if the engine has stopped it's the supply to it that is no longer there. The narrow-gauge garden railway with a Friog Models Harlech Castle is still in place at this time underneath the fiddle yard boards. (March 2010)

Figure 38. The space between the fiddle yard board and house wall is tight. This means that extra tiles from a bathroom project and an MDF board sheet were needed to provide some protection against the operators brushing up against the sandpaper like house bricks and emerging from an operating session considerably thinner than when they went in. There is also a fold-up seat that was meant for a shower, but the operators don't really get the chance to use it as the fiddle yard can be busy. The fiddle yard roof is polycarbonate sheeting. The polycarbonate sheeting comes in a robust plastic sleeve, which makes an ideal false ceiling, cut about a bit, for the fiddle yard and plastic bags filled with plastic bags make a cheap and environmentally sound insulating medium between the false ceiling and roof. (May 2020)

Figure 39. The original configuration of the single-track section was this timber box with hinged top and side. It seemed like a good idea at the time but was soon overtaken by the polycarbonate sheeting. The timber upright that is secured to the concrete fence posts was retained, however. The polycarbonate is less affected by weather, is lighter and cheaper, you can see into it and it provides enough daylight for a camera to operate without lights and yet if you place a light in there you can see it from outside. The timber displaced was recycled into the trackbed for the Watery Road Yard extension. (April 2010)

Figure 40. By 2019 the shed roof at Brymbo East Junction was leaking and a remedy was sought. On eBay they advertise a replacement rubber roof cut to size for the shed roof size you have. The alternative is to strip off the existing mineralised felt, the usual covering, and then refelt using bitumastic adhesive. This is messy and the layout is exposed to the bitumastic and the weather while you are doing it. The roof was covered in the rubber roll supplied with the existing roof left in place. The rubber was secured with around 100 pan head screws fitted underneath the soffit timbers that run round the outside and top of the walls. Expensive adhesive was also specified, but as that had disaster written on it from a layout point of view it was not used. The roof has survived 80-mph winds and all manner of rain and storm that you get in these islands. (March 2020)

Figure 41. The mineralised felt version at Crowndale Halt was only built in 2013 so should last a bit longer. The BEJ shed dates from 2006, so lasted around thirteen years. I've noticed that pigeons are partial to peck the felt and efforts to guide next door's cat up there have been only partially successful. (March 2020)

Track and Points and their Control

The track used is Peco code 124 bullhead rail, as that was similar to what it was in 1936. There is still bullhead rail on Network Rail today, though not on main lines.

A top tip for track laying is to remove or chamfer the sharp edges around the top and sides of the rail to ensure a smooth passage of vehicles over any track joint, particularly those on a curve. A healthy gap will ensure that joints don't close up in hot weather. Track outside can reach 40° C as opposed to, say, 25° C in a dwelling. The gap accentuates the noise of stock running over it but will limit the top speed, which is not such an issue on single-track branch lines.

Ballast is 4 mm scale or OO gauge, as O-gauge ballast is too coarse mixed in with dyed sawdust or static grass on sidings.

The points are also Electrofrog Peco, mostly LH and RH, but there are two large radius points on curves and an SMP 3 waypoint in Watery Road Yard. There is a scratch-built trap point (popularly called a catch point). All track joints are bonded whether they have a fishplate on them or not, but not if the joint is meant to isolate electrically.

Every point – whether manual or electrically controlled – has a separate switching device to switch the point frog polarity. Point blades will work at first but will rapidly prove to be unreliable over a short time. Points that would be manually operated on the prototype have the lever and guard rail modelled.

There is a sector plate in the fiddle yard, and that is scratch built. Point rodding on the scenic sections has been modelled, including facing point lock rodding where appropriate.

Figure 42. All trackwork on the scenic parts of the layout have been sprayed matt black, with chairs and the rail sides picked out in rust. The ramp over the tie bar was made from an aluminium drink can and was used to stop dangling couplings ripping up point mechanisms on the prototype. Occasionally an additional check rail is required, and one is seen modelled after the bridge. Sometimes point blades need chamfering and the stock rail recessing a bit more to suit a particular location. (October 2013)

Figure 43. The tracks reading from left to right at Brymbo East Junction are: passenger-carrying line for the platform, goods and loop line, loco stabling road. The purpose of the trap point in the middle of the picture is to protect the passenger-carrying line and it works in concert with the point that connects passenger and goods lines. On the prototype this is achieved with point rodding, which has been modelled, but in model form there is a separate point motor. Catch points are used where runaway vehicles on gradients usually against the normal direction of travel are derailed. (March 2020)

Figure 44. The top point is set for the goods loop and the trap point moves in concert. The track joint after the trap point is a double break and the rails are held in position by inserting panel pins and soldering the rails to the pins to enable precise levelling. The point on the far left is passenger carrying and therefore has two point rods going to it. There is an extra one for the facing point lock. (March 2020)

Figure 45. Underneath the board at the BEJ station throat and the original point actuating mechanism designed to operate from a slot cut into the baseboard with a piece of brass wire soldered to the longitudinal brass wire. The drawback is that the throw is not easily adjustable, and in O gauge it might need to be. These were only used in the station area at BEJ. (February 2020)

Figure 46. A much-used Fulgurex point motor installed at Crowndale Halt. The brass wire at the end of the copper actuating rod is a cranked piece that goes up through the baseboard in a tube and operates the point tie bar. The copper rod was stripped out of old mains cable earth. The two securing Philips screws are in line with the black actuating slide and if you put in any more there can be a tendency to warp and twist the slide. This makes the motor slow to operate and it takes a lot of current and may eventually jam and burn out the motor. The two micro-switch operating lugs have shoulders moulded onto them. Paring down these shoulders increases the throw somewhat. (March 2020)

Figure 47. On the baseboard top the point actuating lever is the darker rust-coloured rod on the left. This is much longer than the item below the baseboard, Figure 46, and it is the leverage that enlarges the throw of the Fulgurex point motor. You don't have to create a slot in the baseboard. (March 2020)

Figure 48. The biggest single problem with Fulgurex point motors is that eventually the limit micro-switches that stop the motor when it gets to its fullest extent of travel fail open circuit. You can see here that the brass screw turned by the motor has been epoxied into position after a switch failure destroyed the plastic moulding holding it in. This can also lead to a motor burn out. In addition, the micro-switches have been replaced by sealed items from eBay secured in position by eight BA nuts and bolts after carefully drilling a new hole. You can use this method to increase throw as well. The ancillary switches used to operate frogs can be paralleled up to the limit switches and these will double the service life to around ten years. After that it's the new micro-switches.

Connected to the point motor terminals are sealed relays to operate the point frog and these are unaffected by outside climatic conditions and very reliable. (March 2020)

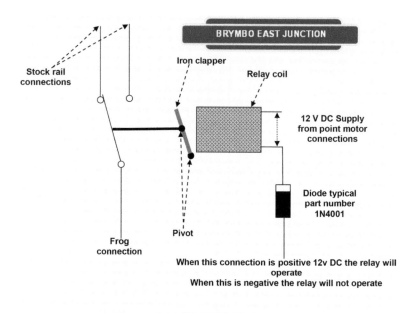

Stock rail connections

Iron clapper

Relay coil

12 V DC Supply from point motor connections

Diode typical part number 1N4001

Pivot

Frog connection

When this connection is positive 12v DC the relay will operate
When this is negative the relay will not operate

Frog Relay

Use of the diode means the relay will only energise on one selection of the point motor as required
You connect as shown and swap the stock rail connections round until it works.
The point motor reverses direction by reversing the polarity of the 12v DC supply.

Figure 49 shows the wiring diagram for a point motor frog relay. The point motor works by applying 12 v DC to the terminals, then to reverse the motor the polarity is reversed.

Figure 50. Above baseboard level a simple crank can be fabricated from brass sheet with an actuating arm of no particular dimensions so long as it fits and has holes drilled in it. As long as the crank at the motor end is nearer the pivot than the tie bar end there will be throw magnification. Note the four cables: two for the supply and two to the frog relay. (March 2020)

Figure 51. Just up from the three-way point is this example where the crank is angled. The blister packaging provides an effective cover and the black plastic cover on the right houses the frog relays. (March 2020)

Figure 52. The five manually operated points in the fiddle yard must have their frogs switched and this is performed by a sealed micro-switch mounted on a strip of brass and secured with ten BA nuts and bolts. The point tie bar is moved across and so operates the switch plunger, which is just about visible. This must be a precise operation and, while the point tie bar and track must not move longitudinally, the micro-switch base is adjustable by the Philips screw on the left. The more it is screwed in, the more it moves the switch base to the right by a very small amount. (March 2020)

Figure 53. The sector plate in the fiddle yard is a sheet of aluminium (the trader on eBay will cut it to size for you) with copper-clad track epoxied to the base. It is pivoted at one end and so describes an arc when you move it. The black cable at the rear is a permanent connection; the other rail is connected by the plug and cable. The black holes on the baseboard are brass tubes into which fits the broken-off twist drill that is connected by the beefy cable. The tubes are connected to switchable sections for each track that lines up. This means you cannot have a track lined up that is not connected properly, but you can switch off whatever is on the sector plate and you can drive an engine off the sector plate if the front portion of the loop siding is occupied by another train.

The aluminium plate was modified a bit when the back siding that houses the GWR pickup goods was put in. Sang Cheng 57XX pannier tank, No. 5761 is the current occupant plus up to eight wagons. The stub siding shown connected can accommodate an autotrain or light engine. (March 2020)

Signals and their Control

The taper wooden posts of the GWR signals were found from a job lot on eBay and mostly only the hardwood posts, finials and brass bases were used. A white metal cast kit was also used for one bracket signal.

Arms and backlight covers are MSE products and the lamps scratch built from tube with 1.8-mm LEDs for illumination. Other parts, such as lamp brackets, wire handrails, rods and brackets, were scratch built from brass or, in the case of some of the bracketry from TT-gauge rail, soldered up and brass pinned to the posts.

Figure 54. Six of the thirteen signals controllable by the BEJ operator are on view here. From left to right they are: bay platform starter, platform starter, GWR branch section signal, shunt signal on post, GCR branch section signal and BEJ loop signal.

All signals are interlocked with their respective points so that it is impossible to end up in the wrong place if the signals are used. The shunt signal is used where the signal post has to be passed, but only to shunt as far as the junction point or workman's carriage siding. (March 2020)

Figure 55. LNER N5 No. 5410 shunts a loaded coal train into the headshunt to await an early departure up the GW branch. The shunt signal covers both the headshunt and carriage siding. The whitewashed sighting background for the Crowndale Halt line was frequently used by the GWR and LMS and other railways. The shunt signal is in use at closer range and therefore does not require sighting equipment. (March 2020)

Figure 56. Brymbo East Junction signals as viewed on the monitor from CCTV Camera 5 (Figure 11) at night. The sighting boards are needed here for the operator to make sure the signal has answered the lever. The route is set from the GW to the loop. (November 2012)

Figure 57. The BEJ bracket signal under construction and the lamps under test. The wooden decking had to be drilled to accept the handrail stanchions, which could be soldered to the TT-gauge rail bracket in places and then the handrail soldered to all uprights. (January 2012)

Figure 58. Further on in the process from the above figure. The bracket would typically be connected to the negative for the LED supply to save running too many wires down the post. The LED wiring is varnished copper wire from an old relay coil. Signals are powered by either adapted solenoids or Fulgurex point motors. A servo and feedback printed circuit board was tried but it only lasted four years outside. (January 2012)

Figure 59. There was a brief flirtation with working and lit ground signals, which, although worked, proved to be vulnerable to damage in service. Now ground signals are attached to point tie bars, which is not strictly prototypically accurate, and neither are they lit. This device signalled the way into the BEJ loco road. (September 2013)

Figure 60. The later incarnation of ground signals is this example. It controls exit from the coal train storage sidings and is actuated by the point tie bar. On the prototype it would not operate when a train was entering the sidings and there would be a separate signal for that move. (April 2020)

Figure 61. At Crowndale Halt, the platform starter is on the left and is 'off' for No. 4502 and B Set coaches to return to BEJ and Wrexham General (fiddle yard). The loop starter signal on the right has been shifted over to the right-hand side of the tracks for space reasons. (October 2015)

Figure 62. The goods departure starter signal had to be recessed into the embankment a bit and there is still work to do to fully integrate it into the scene. The loop signal remains 'on' as the freight train crew must pick up the single-line token before proceeding. (October 2017.)

Figure 63. Springside Collett 2251 class No. 2289 brings the empty stock for the Sunday school excursion to Barmouth down the GW branch towards BEJ past the two fixed distant signals signifying a line speed of 40 mph or less. The coaches are by the erstwhile Western Wagon Works. The signals both point the same way as they are then both looking at Camera 6 head on, although they should actually point the other way at this location. (June 2019)

Figure 64. Cast posts are easier in the sense that they can be the negative conductor for the LEDs, rather like a car circuitry. You can also solder brass components with care with low-melt solder. The brass and white metal must be scrupulously clean and I find Fluxite a necessity. The diodes need a 2.2-v power supply. Adjustable low-voltage supplies are from eBay. (October 2009)

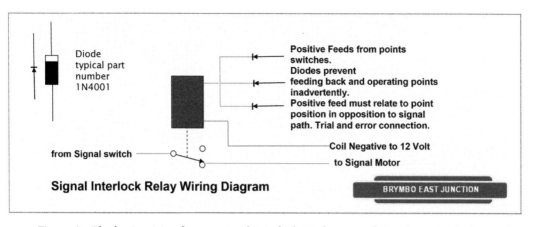

Diode typical part number 1N4001

Positive Feeds from points switches.
Diodes prevent feeding back and operating points inadvertently.
Positive feed must relate to point position in opposition to signal path. Trial and error connection.

Coil Negative to 12 Volt

to Signal Motor

from Signal switch

Signal Interlock Relay Wiring Diagram

BRYMBO EAST JUNCTION

Figure 65. The basic wiring for one signal interlock. Each powered signal needs a lockout relay and there must be a diode with a positive connection from every point motor that the signal needs to be interlocked with. On single lines you may need to interlock signals with other signals that control the opposite direction. In which case you use the positive from a signal supply rather than a point motor and still with a diode for each positive supply. Alternatively, you can construct a lever frame as in real signal box, but that is a huge amount of work and difficult to relock when there are changes.

Structures

There aren't too many buildings on the layout and with two foot-wide scenic boards perhaps it's just as well.

Figure 66. The Churchward Models signal box finished in the GWR structure colours of light and dark stone and fitted with 12-v LED lighting. These are LEDs with an integral resistor to enable a 12-v supply to be used. They are not very reliable in my experience, whereas ordinary LEDs are, provided they get the correct voltage of 2.2 v.

The box has full detail with two single-line token apparatus, which it needs for both branch lines. Since Crowndale Halt was built in 2013 it would need a further set for that line; however, since the line was some distance from the box the token apparatus may have been in the station building or in a lineside cupboard. (April 2008)

Figure 67. The single line out towards Brymbo East Junction itself passes this cluster of corrugated-iron sheds and lamp huts. There should be external single-line token apparatus in the vicinity and that is on the to-do list, although this kit was not always used in reality. (September 2019)

Figure 68. The LNWR signal box at Crowndale Halt was an eBay purchase on a brick base but the location required the box to be elevated, like some of the boxes at Chester General station. This frame and plinth was fabricated from brass section and Plasticard. The point rodding that follows the span was calculated to be correct, taking account of facing point locks and crossover single rods and modelled in brass rod. The signal wires were not modelled but the pulleys can be seen on the right. Note the use of copper-clad strip to keep the point rodding parallel. (February 2014)

Figure 69. Although the signal box body came with a light and full interior detail, the roof was tile paper. In order to give it some body, individual stickers from WHSmith were stuck on to simulate slates. The fact that they are different colours is good in that they appear to be different shades of slate grey when painted and many slate roofs bear this out and have a differing patina depending on how the slate was cleaved. (March 2014)

Figure 70. The completed LNWR box is in service at Crowndale Halt after the installation of point rodding to connect with the boxes. Like Shrewsbury, this joint station has an LNWR box and GWR signals. The overbridge is by Peco. The Sunday school excursion is just disappearing, Move 4. (March 2020)

Figure 71. The former crossing keeper's cottage is typical Shrewsbury & Chester Railway architecture and was to form the basis for the BEJ station building. The signal box behind is Croes Newydd North Fork in Wrexham, which formed part of the triangle of lines that ran up to the steelworks at Brymbo. (April 2019)

Figure 72. Brymbo East Junction station building. It is a balsa wood shell to give stone wall depth, then covered with stone Plasticard for the walls and plain for the window frames. The windows and bargeboards are etched Scale Link products, the interior lighting grain of wheat 12-v bulbs run on 9 v DC. The chimney pots are copper strip (draught excluder) cut with a pair of pinking shears to give the saw tooth effect. The enamel advertising plaques are supplied in a sheet and cut out. (April 2020)

Figure 73. The water tower at Brymbo East Junction is of nowhere in particular except that it fits the cast metal tank. The stone base is of balsa and Plasticard construction except this time there is a slurry of plaster-type filler applied to give the impression of rough-hewn stone rather than the dressed variety of the station building. The corrugated-iron sheets on the roof are a bit ramshackle. The cast kit crane is used to handle permanent way components as the sidings are mainly for holding. (December 2019)

Figure 74. Crowndale Halt station building is typical of a small station lockup and attracts the usual attention from advertisers with enamel signs. The posters have faded somewhat. They are paper photocopies of repro posters scaled down. The plastic Slaters lamps have LEDs in them and look suitably gas or oil like in brightness. The enamel signs have brass sheet backing. (April 2020)

Figure 75. The goods shed is very simple without the usual offices and outbuildings as space would not permit. The LMS pickup goods awaits departure in front of the shed, Move 11, and the track is boarded over for road vehicles by the doors. (April 2020)

Figure 76. The low relief row of railway worker's cottages was made by Malcolm Genner, who is a former member of RAF Sealand Model Railway Club and a noted builder of buildings. The lower light platform lamps are LED replacements for the original grain of wheat bulbs. (April 2020)

Figure 77. Malcolm's attention to detail extends to the *Daily Sketch* newspaper in the outside privy, or WC, of one of the cottages. The back scene is by Gaugemaster. (April 2020)

CHAPTER 4

Railway Vehicles

In terms of coupling, the basic principal was that all vehicles have either screw-link, instanter or three-link couplings where appropriate. It means an over-scale hand coupling and uncoupling, but the hand is only there momentarily whereas 'automatic' couplings look wrong 100 per cent of the time and are not usually 100 per cent reliable. Shunted goods wagons have four link couplings to aid visibility with the bottom link. The operators also find it maintains visual acuity and dextrousness when otherwise these facilities would decline over the years.

Locomotives

The locomotives are from a variety of sources and to acquire twenty-five steam engines just by building them would take most of my time and leave no time to do other things. I have built some of them myself, however, but we are reaching a point where ready-to-run engines mean that self-build is unnecessary and expensive. We have already reached that point with diesel outline locos. They will be dealt with in the rough order of acquisition.

The eBay-purchased items were almost all indifferent runners when bought, but were easily fixed as long as the bodywork was well put together and the engine looked right.

They mostly use Slaters phosphor-bronze wiper pickups on at least six wheels, although Sang Cheng engines have plunger pickups. Most engines have lead ballast to improve traction. Some weathering has been done where a toylike newness was present, but mostly the stock has weathered naturally.

All locos have the lamp code for the train they are pulling/pushing, although only light engines have the correct lamp in the relevant direction of travel.

References to the sequence move will be made if appropriate. Please see Appendix A for operating sequence.

Figure 78. No. 6412 GWR 64XX pannier is a Castle Kits cast kit and uses an ex-MOD coreless motor and Romford 30-1 gears. It is 24 v and is partly the reason we have 0–30-v controllers. Usually works the 163 Autocoach to Plas Power Halt (GC-LNER). Built in 2006. Here seen arriving at Brymbo East Junction, Move 40. (September 2018. Now auto-fitted spare in 2020)

Figure 79. No. 4851 Scorpio mostly etched brass kit with masses of lead in the smokebox and sprung bogie wheel with six-wheel pickup and a 24-v coreless motor. The engine is in 1934 livery. (Shown on Move 6, April 2020)

Figure 80. 1991–2021 Class pannier tank, Eric Underhill kit bought from Merseyside Model Railway Society. Heads up the 205 autocoach that shuttles from Wrexham General (GW) to Crowndale Halt, Move 5. (April 2020)

Figure 81. No. 2743, 27XX Dean Pannier Tank, from MMRS again but scratch built this time. As the engine is only power class A it is limited to such duties as shunting and the workman's train. Coal trains require at least GWR power class C. This type of engine would be long in the tooth in 1936 but some would survive thanks to the Second World War.

Figure 82. No. 7714, 57XX pannier tank, Castle kits from eBay with the Mashima 1833 motor but with 40-1 gears and plenty of lead to handle the steel products train, which is loaded with steel and very heavy, moves 10 and 34. This is the only freight train that runs round and it has to use the platform road as the loop is not long enough. Originally in BR black, but fortunately without BR-era fittings, and resprayed and re-lettered to GWR 1927 green livery. (September 2018)

Figure 83. No. 8701, 57XX pannier tank, Castle kits from eBay with the Mashima 1833 motor and 30-1 gears. There are five engines dedicated to coal trains in addition. This is the spare, depicted at its usual spot on the loco road at BEJ complete with headcode, front and rear. (April 2020)

Figure 84. No. 5687, GWR 56XX 0-6-2T was another eBay purchase from a guy who used to fire the real thing in South Wales. The last working 56XX were at Croes Newydd, Wrexham so this engine is not out of place. It is powered by a Bühler motor and is 40-1 geared so is a real hauler. The train of empties has arrived from the GW by a loco that is the other side of the bridge. No. 5687 has backed onto the rear of the train and is now waiting for the loop signal to head up the GC branch to Plas Power Colliery, Move 22. (April 2020)

Figure 85. No. 5764, 57XX Scorpio kit shunts the short parcels train into the bay siding to access the end loading dock after it has run round the train on arrival, Move 25. The steel products train in the foreground is stored until a path can be found between coal trains. (July 2019)

Figure 86. No. 4588, GWR 4575 Class (Tower Models) Sang Cheng – superb detailing and performance and no plastic parts, Dennis Morley painted. This engine heads up the clerestory coach excursion to Llanberis via Chester where the engine is changed. This train is buried within Watery Road Yard outside until Move 40 when it is brought out for departure. The photograph beyond the engine details the order in which trains must go to be ready for next week but all inside the fiddle yard shed. (April 2020)

Figure 87. Nos 5410 and 5548 LNER (ex-GCR) N5 0-6-2T under construction, both Haywood Railway kits. The engines have pivoted brake gear with plastic shoes, so a useful non-short-circuit feature. Both engines were allocated to Wrexham Rhosddu LNER shed in the 1930s. (January 2010)

Figure 88. LNER N5 5410 awaits departure from BEJ with Move 20, Vauxhall/Cambrian loaded coal train down the GW branch to the steelworks. The coal train engines come off the working at BEJ and then back on to take the next arrival. This means they swap around all the time and you need five engines to work four trains, but you don't have to keep running round at BEJ, thereby maintaining the flow of traffic for the other two operators. (January 2013)

Figure 89. LNER N5 5548 is in the fiddle yard and heading the United National/Mixed wagon loaded coal train, Move 7. (April 2020)

Figure 90. No. 4502, GWR 45XX class, Springside kit has the 'off' for Brymbo East Junction with the Wrexham No. 3 B Set. This eBay engine needed springing on both bogie wheelsets, new pickups, crosshead driven vacuum pump and slide bar bracket fabricated from TT-gauge rail as opposed to cast ones, Move 26. (March 2015)

Figure 91. No. 2785, 27XX scratch built from eBay, pickups changed. Now standby engine at Crowndale Halt and hides behind the goods shed. (April 2020)

Figure 92. No. 7459 LMS Jinty 0-6-0T, kit built from eBay with compensation and Bühler motor, fitted pickups, very slow runner. Originally bought for LMS pickup goods, now Crowndale Halt yard shunter. (September 2019)

Figure 93. LMS Fowler 4F, Sang Cheng from eBay as bought in BR livery. Slipping driving wheels on axles initially cured with axle slots and brass wire. Eventually wheels and axles replaced with Slaters. Tender modified to pickup from four wheels. (November 2013)

Figure 94. No. 4539 LMS Fowler 4F awaits a departure with the twice-sequence LMS pickup goods from Crowndale Halt. (June 2015)

Figure 95. No. 4570 45XX small prairie scratch built from eBay. Needed pickups and eventually remotored after around five years as the worn Portescap gear box failed. (April 2020)

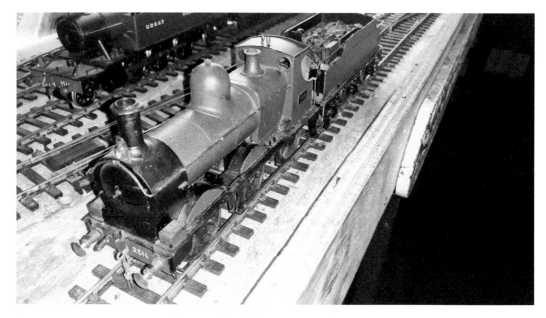

Figure 96. No. 2516 Dean Goods, scratch built from eBay and retains its Portescap motor and gearbox but with tender pickups. Limited to the workman's four wheelers, excursion empty stock downhill or GW pickup goods. (April 2020)

Figure 97. No. 5322 Churchward Mogul, eBay scratchbuilt, remotored with Mashima 1833 and Romford 30-1 gears from Portescap, heads the Sunday school excursion from Crowndale Halt, Move 4, light engine code lamp on tender. (April 2020)

Figure 98. No. 2287, 2251 Class, eBay Springside kit, Collett intermediate tender with pickups added waits at the loop signal for the GW road back to the fiddle yard. It had brought the excursion empty stock to Crowndale Halt, Move 48. The Collett will pass the Mogul train engine for the excursion on the GC line. (November 2019)

Figure 99. No. 2259, 2251 Class Martin Finney kit under construction. This kit was like building a real loco; there are many parts not found on other kits. Fits together very well and excellent instructions, Churchward 3,500-gl tender only supplied so it has to be one of the earlier numbered series. Modified to cope with sharp curves and tender pickups. (November 2015)

Figure 100. No. 2259, kit completed and waiting to be paired up with a brace of Collett coaches from Western Wagon Works and usually a van to work to Oswestry over the Great Central branch to Wrexham Central, Move 3. (March 2016)

Figure 101. No. 5922, LNER N5 0-6-2T, Haywood Railway, brings its loaded coal train into the holding sidings awaiting its turn for the GW branch, Move 44 then Move 8 the following week. This eBay engine was nicely made and ran well and only needed new pickups to enter service. (April 2020)

Figure 102. No. 5761, Sang Cheng from eBay, noisy gears quietened, is heading to GWR pickup goods, Move 37, in the departure siding at Crowndale Halt. The top feed was a later addition so is incorrect for the period. Dennis Morley painted. (May 2019)

Figure 103. No. 2769 27XX class, Scorpio Models kit with workman's train of four wheelers at BEJ, Move 2 and returns on 46. The train has been shunted into the goods loop to let another passenger train access to the platform. Scorpio kits always include masses of parts so that you can build every conceivable variant in the class or use the excess on other engines. (November 2012)

Figure 104. No. 5181, 51XX large prairie, Heljan. A few modifications: bunker piled up with coal, silver paint on buffer shanks, rust on rods, cab roof opened. This engine has filled in with a coal train, Move 15, and now waits for the returning Barmouth excursion. The tender of the 4F is just visible with the last returning LMS pickup so this is Move 45. (November 2019)

Figure 105. No. 5172, 51XX large prairie, Heljan. This engine stopped on plain track with 0 A on the ammeter and it was not commanded to stop. Fabricated a piece of printed circuit board strip and phosphor bronze pickups with brass hooks to secure crocodile clips when wheel cleaning. Shown passing Watery Road Yard with the Barmouth excursion with DAPOL B set coaches, Move 1. (April 2020)

Figure 106. No. 5000, LMS Black 5 is from an ancient Jamieson (E.A.M.E.S.) kit with some more modern fittings. The major components are at variance with the drawing, so this is just like scratch building. Haven't thought of a job for this engine yet but there's plenty of time for that. Workbench tidied. (January 2020)

Diesels

Figure 107. The layout and stock remain the same on diesel nights so we have taper post signals and private owner and private company wagons and the structures in either GWR or LMS colours, but this cannot be helped. The Crowndale Halt branch is closed and traffic concentrates on coal trains, transfer freights and the odd DMU.

Diesels are mostly Heljan with renowned haulage and detail properties but some of the plastic small detail is vulnerable. Apart from numbering and Western Region route availability discs for certain classes, even though this part of the system was London Midland Region from September 1963 they have only had the silver paint on the buffer shanks treatment. The single-car DMU has been remotored and pickups fitted to all wheels and the excellent DAPOL 08 is as bought. (March 2020)

Figure 108. Heljan Class 33 Crompton D6534 makes its way on the LNER branch with a train of coal empties on a diesel evening. (May 2019)

Figure 109. The Class 47, D1648, waits for the GW branch signal with a twenty-wagon loaded coal train while the steam stock is furloughed for the evening. (November 2014)

Figure 110. The DAPOL 08 diesel shunter confidently grapples with twenty-six wagons on the 1 in 60 gradient. Note tiny headlight. (December 2016)

Figure 111. M79901 Single Diesel Railcar has a test run after the motor bogie was revamped and pickups fitted to all wheels. (March 2014.)

Figure 112. D5054 Class 24 was one of the original diesel classes on the Brymbo branch, but almost always in pairs. Fortunately, the model is a dual-motored Bachman Brass item. (July 2009)

Rolling Stock

Passenger coaches are mostly from the Western Wagon Works stable who is no longer in business, but he produced a reasonable standard of model at affordable prices and they have proved to be reliable in service. One of the best features are the roofs, which are built up of strip and covered with tissue, which most closely resembles the way the coaches were actually built. DAPOL coaches are rich in detail but not price, and have lighting which on a DC layout tend to flicker like the old Trix coaches and go out when the train stops – one up for DCC here. The couplings are scale and this means they have to be supplemented by brass chain to get round sharp curves.

There are etched coaches by the extinct Mallard Models and they run and look well.

Freight wagons are a mixture with the coal trains being basically Powsides, Parkside, DAPOL with Slaters, Peco or Parkside brake vans. The empty coal train wagons have a small lead weight underneath, but full wagons rely on the load of coal. The difference in the way empty and full trains behave is quite striking. Coal trains are in four set rakes of eight wagons and two brake vans – two full, two empty.

Other wagons are by Scorpio, etched kits that are very comprehensive but take a while to build. Other makes are DAPOL, Peco, Parkside and Slaters.

Some wagons have a brake shoe in the 'on' position, which makes the characteristic squealing noise of a beaten-up private-owner wagon with grease axle boxes. The train also 'hunts' as the freewheeling wagons bang spring buffers with the retarded ones. Some wagons, other than brake vans, that are the end vehicles in passenger and van trains are equipped with tail lamps.

CHAPTER 5

Control and Block Instruments

The layout is DC controlled as opposed to DCC, and while conversion to DCC has been talked about the amount of work involved does not justify the benefits received, although I have to say that the addition of locomotive sounds adds a dimension to the hobby if it is done well.

I feel in 2020 that DCC is in the same position as electric cars – they are a work in progress. DCC would be improved if a locomotive were equipped with an infrared sensor you simply pointed the 'remote' at, or if the whole layout were depicted on a touch screen and locos could be similarly selected – even if they are not in view – by the operator. Also, I am not keen on the system cutting out and carrying out a reboot for some trivial occurrence.

The controllers are all stabilised power supplies as used in electronics laboratories and workshops that maintain a constant selected voltage supply irrespective of the load. The usual maximum voltage is 30 as there are some 24-v mechanisms.

They all have instrumentation of voltage and particularly current, which is useful to establish what is happening to the engine even if you can't see it. They lack a reversing switch, which is easily overcome but all have short-circuit protection and range from 3 amperes (A) maximum load, which is plenty for a Heljan Class 47 with twenty wagons ascending the 1 in 60, which takes around 1.75 A and later controller models are 5 A maximum load. They are also considerably cheaper than commercial model railway controllers.

Figure 113. Brymbo East Junction control panel was built around a commercial lockable box as it was thought it would be used on an exhibition layout. Functionality has much increased over the years.

Point levers have black sleeves and home signals red, as in a real signal box. The route is set for a train to leave the platform and go along the GW branch, as can be seen from both the point selections and the signals S1 and S4. The controller reversing switch has the blue surround. Most of the 12-v LEDs that indicate selection only lasted around five years in service, so the completion of their installation was abandoned.

The UP designation refers to the line direction, which is up towards Wrexham General and coincidentally and unprototypically it is also 1 in 60 up. (April 2020)

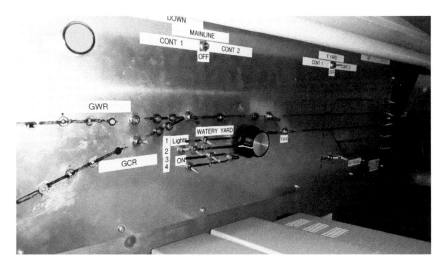

Figure 114. The control panel at the fiddle yard is a sheet of aluminium cut to size by the trader on eBay and then a wooden frame made with holes drilled. The yellow button activates Controller 1, if selected, to transition a train between the two controllers. The two switches at the top enable either controller to operate the main line or fiddle yard in the event of a controller malfunction. The green light indicates that the GW section is off, whereas the two red lights below indicate that not only is the GC section live but that the point to gain access is also in the correct position. The rotary switch is for the three-way point and that needs diodes to ensure that the correct number and orientation of point motors operate for the selection made. The black permanent felt tip pen for the track wears off after a few years and needs refreshing. (April 2020)

Figure 115. Of the controllers at the fiddle yard, Controller 2 has a train – it's a Heljan Prairie. This and the four DAPOL coaches are heading for Brymbo East Junction. The voltage is as selected but the current (lower reading) is what the train is taking, 0.58 A. This means the train hasn't reached the 1 in 60 downhill section where the current will reduce. This value includes DAPOL coach lighting; clearly if the train were ascending the gradient the current would be much more. Controller 1 will need to be set to roughly the same value of voltage or less to take over going downhill, and the yellow button will be pressed for a few seconds while the train is in that sub-section. Camera 7 (Figure 11) can be selected to show the changeover point. After the changeover the train can proceed on its own until it either reaches the BEJ handover point or is isolated on one of the fiddle yards sections. This frees up the fiddle yard operator to prepare or shunt the next moves. The journey will take two minutes for a slow freight train.

The 12-v power supply on the right is for points, relays and lights down to the actual junction, which is around 70 feet away. (April 202)

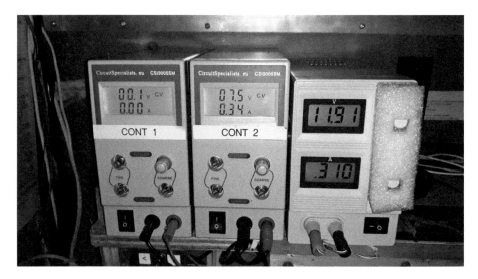

Figure 116. The Heljan Prairie and train start to go down the 1 in 60 and the reduction on the current is telling. (April 2020)

Figure 117. The Crowndale Halt control panel with the aluminium panel exposed. The Emmental cheese-looking object is a 24-v power supply for the signals and the small, printed circuit board is the signal interlock board with three relays and a number of diodes on it. LNWR block instrument is at the top left, the stanchions on the base make ideal wiring conduits. (September 2015)

Absolute Block Operations

The line uses double-track block instruments whereas all the running lines are single track. The reasons are that single-line block instruments are very large and usually a full-size token would have to be carried on the engine in order for it to be handed in at the destination, which then acts to authorise a contra movement.

Clearly this would be impossible on the model, and the instruments themselves are ferociously expensive on the second-hand market. They are so scarce that Network Rail have awarded contracts (in 2019) for the construction of new token apparatus after the Tyer's type.

The double-track block instruments are adapted such that the single lines are organised into UP and DOWN directions. This means what is supposed to be separate tracks are in fact one and the same, only the direction of travel is different.

To pass a stopping passenger train from BEJ to Wrexham General (fiddle yard), GWR, the sequence is as follows (dot indicates a pause):

Figure 118. The 'block shelf' at Brymbo East Junction shed. From the left are the Crowndale Halt set with a mushroom block bell and ancient Spagnoletti block. Then the Great Central (LNER) with a 1947 GW block (ex-Bedwyn) and cow bell. Finally, there is the GW section, which has another 1947 block with church bell. The three different block bells sound distinct, so the operator knows who is calling. The two home signal indicators actually replicate the GW and GC branch starter's position. The two distant yellow indicators give fiddle yard section status as distant signals are fixed on the layout.

BEJ		Fiddle Yard	
Activity	Bell Code	Activity	Bell Code
Call Attention	1	Acknowledge	1
Line clear for passenger train?	3.1	Acknowledge Line is clear for passenger train (selects Line Clear which is reflected on upper section at BEJ block)	3.1
Train entering block section	2 (Handover point)	Acknowledge Train entereing block section (selects Train on Line which is reflected on upper section at BEJ block)	2
Train out of section	2.1	Train Out of Section (upon arrival at fiddle yard) Selects Normal on block, reflected at BEJ block	2.1

There are other bell codes used if something is wrong; for example, if a train divides in section.

Figure 119. The block instruments don't have to be railway relics, they can be knocked up from lights and switches as the fiddle yard here. There is a further switch round the side to select GW or GC route. This block is reflecting the position outlined in the table where the GW train was offered by BEJ and accepted by the fiddle yard. The instrument next to the block is a GC indicator only and BEJ have accepted a train and given Line Clear. This reflected on the BR 'domino' moving coil meter instrument. Next to that is the art deco loudspeaker for the halfway microphone.

Figure 120. Some of what has been selected on the instruments is seen to be unfolding outside on Camera 6, near the junction, and depicted on the small monitor on the left. The GC block is showing Train On Line, which is referring to the 163 Autocoach on the right, Move 24. While on the small Spagnoletti block it is showing Line Clear on the GW (vans Move 25). (April 2018)

Figure 121. The LNWR block instrument at Crowndale Halt is again an adapted double-line machine and has the block bell integral to the unit. (April 2020)

CHAPTER 6

Closed-circuit Television

CCTV is essential on a layout where the entire outdoor track is not visible to the operators directly and trains need to be controlled instead of orbiting.

The basic elements of the CCTV system are very simple and it can all be bought from eBay inexpensively. The cameras are mostly of the miniature type, around £8, 12-v powered and with the white, yellow and red phono connections as you find on a home TV or audio system. They have infrared LEDs for night use, but you may need additional lighting.

To avoid the layout looking like Mission Control at Houston, the monitor size, or lack of it, is an important consideration.

The monitors are mostly of the type that have two video inputs and are around the size of a satnav in a car. The monitors are designed to display an in-car DVD or the view from a reversing camera but are manually selectable. They too have the phono connections previously described. In 2020 they were around £25, but they look after two cameras.

The snag is the cable, readily available, is described as BNC or Bayonet Neill–Concelman to honour its designers. This uses co-axial cable rather like a terrestrial TV cable and bayonet connections rather like a British light bulb. This means you have to buy adapters for phono to BNC wherever you need to connect a camera to a monitor; however they are cheap on eBay – around 50p each.

The 12-v power supplies need to be of around 2 A rating, but this depends how many cameras and monitors you have. It needs to be of the laptop type to keep electrical noise down otherwise it will appear on the CCTV screen as interference. Once again, eBay sells these items – a 12-v 5-A power supply is around £10.

The only other device needed is a BNC T piece to split video onto different monitors.

There is one monitor that is basically a cheap 14-in TV that needs a detailed view of signals so operators can give Train Out of Section on the block bell by spotting the tail lamp of a train.

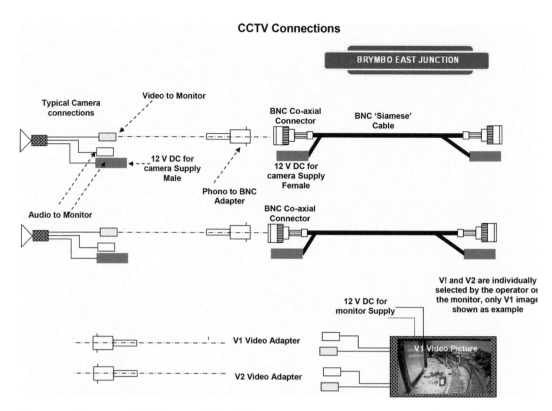

Figure 122. Diagram of CCTV connectivity. All components except 12-v power supplies are shown.

Figure 123. The tail lamp monitor, which also gives feedback as to signal position. The GW branch signal is 'OFF' or go together with the loop signal on the bracket. This view is replicated at the fiddle yard, Camera 5. (April 2015)

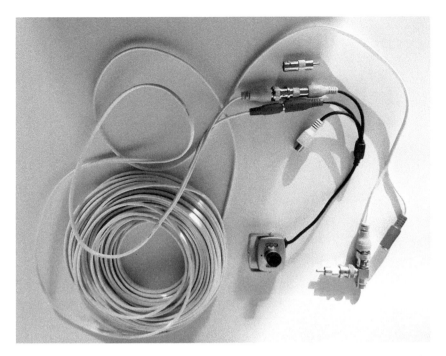

Figure 124. Depicts 10 metres of BNC cable connected to a miniature camera with adapters and a T-piece to take the video off to a different shed. The 12-v power supply plugs in to the vacant red connector inside the shed. The white audio connector is unused. (May 2020)

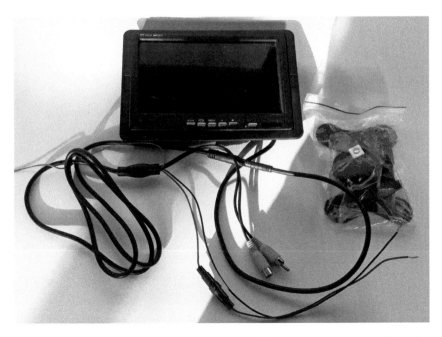

Figure 125. The two-view monitor shows its two yellow video inputs as well as the 12-v DC input cables – red and black. Green is unused as it to do with switching video when reversing a car. The swivel mount is included in the package. (May 2020)

Figure 126. Camera 7 looks back up towards the fiddle yard from Watery Road Yard. There must be two cameras in the yard as stock will block the view from one camera. Operators prefer looking at the monitor when it is -5° C, and especially when it is torrentially raining outside. Coats are provided. (April 2015)

Figure 127. The view from Camera 7 with the lid down and the yard uncharacteristically empty. The monitor is also used for looking at Camera 5 by the GW and GC markings. Both monitor's views are arranged in pairs so that the yard is one set on two monitors and the junction another. (September 2015)

CHAPTER 7
Photo Gallery

Although quite a lot of the layout has been depicted in the book so far, what follows is a further selection to fill any gaps.

Figure 128. A sunny March 2017 and Watery Road Yard is quite busy, and this is in addition to the five loops within the fiddle yard shed. A loaded coal train on the right is under Fiddle Yard Controller 2, having passed the changeover point.

Figure 129. Still March 2017 and 4502 and B Set coaches head for Wrexham General on the GW while a loaded coal train from Plas Power Colliery heads for Brymbo East Junction on the LNER (GC) branch. The parts of the layout that are under CCTV coverage are scenicked to a degree.

Figure 130. The local inspector is about to use the barrow crossing at BEJ, but not until the LMS 4F has gone past with the first of the day's pickup goods. (December 2013)

Figure 131. No. 4851 brings the workman's train of four-wheeled coaches into the platform. It will run round and store the coaches in a purpose-built siding outside the shed, Move 2. It alternates on this duty with No. 2516 as well as No. 6412 and the 163 Autocoach in the background. (February 2014)

Figure 132. Outside the BEJ shed is a carriage siding holding No. 5181 and Birmingham four-coach B Set for the Barmouth excursion, No. 5172 on a fill-in loaded coal train for the steelworks, and on the Crowndale Halt branch line another freight has arrived and will be shunted into one of the holding sidings. (December 2018)

Figure 133. The block shelf at BEJ reveals what is happening outside. The LNER Plas Power box (fiddle yard) has accepted a train that is on its way. BEJ has accepted a train on the GW and that is making its much shorter journey towards the station.

The incoming GW signal has been put back to danger, so the train is about at the workman's carriage siding, Camera 4. The trains have passed each other on the loop effectively. (November 2018)

Figure 134. No. 2259 Martin Finney Collett with Collett coaches and Mica A van wait for the off to take the train down the LNER to Wrexham Central and then over the former Cambrian to Oswestry, Move 3. No. 4851 waits in the bay with the shuttle to Plas Power Halt also over the LNER branch.

Figure 135. A conversation piece is about to be interrupted by the inspector making his way over from the station. The signalman's bike will be quite safe there. The S&T plates were an early form of text message to let either the signalling technician or telegraph lineman know they were needed. (April 2020)

Figure 136. The LNER N5 5922 eases its loaded coal train into one of the holding sidings before heading up the GW to the steelworks. (April 2020)

Figure 137. The block shelf at the fiddle yard before the start of the sequence and before some of the stock is moved outside into the yard. (April 2020)

Figure 138. Move 1 and Heljan large prairie 5172 will take the GW branch eventually with the Barmouth excursion. The clerestories with No. 4588 in the yard will be joined by the steel products train and the 205 Autocoach to allow free movement and run round in the fiddle yard. (April 2020)

Figure 139. Crowndale Halt and while the No. 2251 Class Collett 2289 awaits the road light engine, the Fowler 4F is arriving with the last LMS pickup goods of the day. (November 2016)

Figure 140. No. 4502 and the Wrexham No. 3 B Set have the road to Crowndale Halt with a local service, Move 23. The family are still train spotting on the bridge. (April 2020)

Appendix A

Brymbo East Junction Working Sequence, April 2018

No.	Orig	Branch	Bell	Description	Onward	Notes
1	FY	GWR	4	4 Coach B Set	Prairie back on	Birmingham to Barmouth
2	FY	GWR	1.3	Workman's 4 wheel		RunRound-CS, S1,S5
3	BEJ	GCR	3.1	Collett pair + van	(loco 2259)	Wrexham C to Oswestry
4	CH	LNW/GW	4	Excursion Barmouth	GWR 4	Mogul + 3 coaches
5	FY	GWR	3.1.3	Autocoach 205	LNW/GW 3.1.3	Platform to CH
6	BEJ	GCR	3.1.3	Autocoach 163		Next move 13
7	FY	GCR	1.2	CT Utd Nat/ Mixed		Next move 15
8	BEJ	GWR	3	CT Vaux/Camb		Next move 17
9	BEJ	GCR	1.2	CT E Min/ Broughton		Next move 19
10	FY	GWR	3	Steel Products		To BEJ sidings
11	CH	LNW/GW	3	LMS Pickup Goods	GCR 1.2	Next move 16
12	FY	GWR	3.1	Wrexham No. 3 B Set	LNW/GW 3.1	Next move 14
13	FY	GCR	3.1.3	Autocoach 163		Connects with B Set at BEJ

14	CH	LNW/GW	3.1	Wrexham No. 3 B Set	GWR 3.1	Next move 26
15	BEJ	GWR	3	CT Utd Nat/ Mixed		Next move 27
16	FY	GCR	1.2	LMS Pickup Goods	LNW/GW 3	Next move 30
17	FY	GCR	1.2	CT Vauxhall/ Camb		Next move 20
18	CH	LNW/GW	3.1.3	Autocoach 205	GWR 3.1.3	Oswestry via Wrxhm Gen
19	FY	GWR	4.1	CT E Min/ Broughton		Next move 22
20	BEJ	GWR	3	CT Vaux/Camb		Next move 44
21	FY	GWR	4.1	CT E Vaux/ Gresford		Next move 29
22	BEJ	GCR	1.2	CT E Min/ Broughton		Next move 35
23	FY	GWR	3.1	Wrexham No. 3 B Set	LNW/GW 3.1	Connects with Auto at BEJ
24	BEJ	GCR	3.1.3	Autocoach 163		Next move 40
25	FY	GWR	5	Vans + Siphon F		2 Vans Max, to Bay
26	CH	LNW/GW	3.1	Wrexham No. 3 B Set	GWR 3.1	NEXT MOVE NEXT WEEK
27	FY	GCR	1.2	CT United Natl/ Mix		Next move 32
28	FY	GWR	3.1.3	Autocoach 205	LNW/GW 3.1.3	Next move 36
29	BEJ	GCR	1.2	CT E Vaux/ Gresford		Next move 33
30	CH	LNW/GW	3	LMS Pickup Goods	GCR 1.2	Next move 45
31	FY	GWR	3	GWR Pickup Goods	LNW/GW 3	- C Halt, shunt wagons
32	BEJ	GWR	3	CT Utd Nat/ Mixed		NEXT MOVE NEXT WEEK
33	FY	GWR	4.1	CT E Vaux/ Gresford		Next move 42
34	BEJ	GCR	1.2	Steel Products		Chester, CLC, Manchstr

35	FY	GWR	4.1	CT E Minera/ Brghtn		NEXT MOVE NEXT WEEK
36	CH	LNW/GW	3.1.3	Autocoach 205	GWR 3.1.3	NEXT MOVE NEXT WEEK
37	CH	LNW/GW	1.2	GWR Pickup Goods	GCR 1.2	NEXT MOVE NEXT WEEK
38	BEJ	GCR	5	Vans, Siphon F		NEXT MOVE NEXT WEEK
39	FY	GWR	4	Clerestory Excursion		Platform Run round
40	FY	GCR	3.1.3	Autocoach 163		NEXT MOVE NEXT WEEK
41	BEJ	GWR	4	Clerestory Excursion		For Llanberis & Snowdon
42	BEJ	GCR	1.2	CT E Vaux/ Gresford		NEXT MOVE NEXT WEEK
43	FY	GWR	2.2.1	Excursion ECS	LNW/GW 2.2.1	Collett 2289
44	FY	GCR	1.2	CT Vaux/Camb		NEXT MOVE NEXT WEEK
45	FY	GCR	1.2	LMS Pickup Goods	LNW/GW 3	NEXT MOVE NEXT WEEK
46	BEJ	GWR	1.3	Workman's 4 wheel		From CS to Platform
47	FY	GCR	3.1	Dean/Collett pair + van		Wrexham C from Oswtry
48	CH	LNW/GW	2.3	Dean/Collett from ECS	GWR 2.3	Collett to Croes Newydd
49	FY	GCR	2.3	Mogul for Excursion	LNW/GW 2.3	
50	BEJ	GWR	4	4 Coach B set	Prairie back on	Birmingham to Barmouth

CT = Coal Train, CT E = Coal Train Empties, LNW/GW = The line from BEJ to CH Crowndale Halt, CS = Carriage Siding